children's HISTORY of YORK

Written by
Sarah Freeman

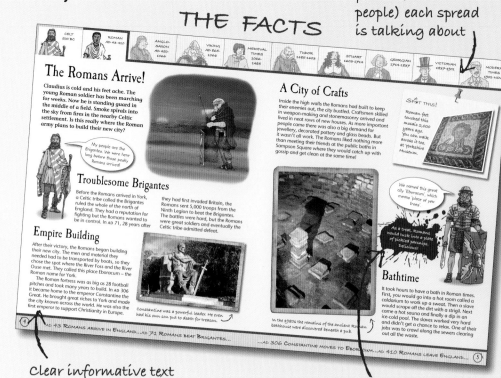

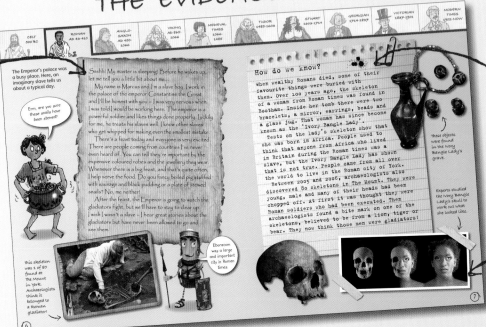

How well do you know your town?

Have you ever wondered what it would have been like living in York when the Vikings arrived? What about being a wigmaker for all the rich people in Tudor times? This book tells the story of your town, with all the important and exciting things that have happened there.

Want to hear the other good bits? You will love this book! Some rather brainy folk have worked on it to make sure it's fun and informative. So what are you waiting for? Peel back the pages and be amazed at what happened in your town.

Timeline shows which period (dates and people) each spread is talking about

THE FACTS

Clear informative text

Hometown facts to amaze you!

THE EVIDENCE

Go back in time to read what it was like for children growing up in York.

Each period in the book ends with a summary explaining how we know about the past.

Exciting historical images

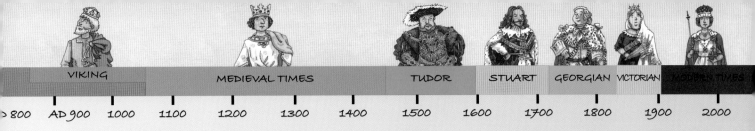

Contents

CELT
500 BC

ROMAN
AD 43-410

ANGLO-
SAXON
AD 450-
1066

VIKING
AD 865-
1066

MEDIEV
TIME
1066
1485

The Romans Arrive!

Claudius is cold and his feet ache. The young Roman soldier has been marching for weeks. Now he is standing guard in the middle of a field. Smoke spirals into the sky from fires in the nearby Celtic settlement. Is this really where the Roman army plans to build their new city?

My people are the Brigantes. We were here long before those pesky Romans arrived!

Troublesome Brigantes

Before the Romans arrived in York, a Celtic tribe called the Brigantes ruled the whole of the north of England. They had a reputation for fighting but the Romans wanted to be in control. In AD 71, 28 years after they had first invaded Britain, the Romans sent 5,000 troops from the Ninth Legion to beat the Brigantes. The battles were hard, but the Romans were great soldiers and eventually the Celtic tribe admitted defeat.

Empire Building

After their victory, the Romans began building their new city. The men and material they needed had to be transported by boats, so they chose the spot where the River Foss and the River Ouse met. They called this place Eboracum – the Roman name for York.

The Roman fortress was as big as 28 football pitches and took many years to build. In AD 306 it became home to the emperor Constantine the Great. He brought great riches to York and made the city known across the world. He was also the first emperor to support Christianity in Europe.

Constantine was a powerful leader. He even had his own son put to death for treason.

4

AD 43 ROMANS ARRIVE IN ENGLAND...AD 71 ROMANS BEAT BRIGANTES...

TUDOR
1485-1603

STUART
1603-1714

GEORGIAN
1714-1837

VICTORIAN
1837-1901

MODERN
TIMES
1902-NOW

A City of Crafts

Inside the high walls the Romans had built to keep their enemies out, the city bustled. Craftsmen skilled in weapon-making and stonemasonry arrived and lived in neat rows of new houses. As more important people came there was also a big demand for jewellery, decorated pottery and glass beads. But it wasn't all work. The Romans liked nothing more than meeting their friends at the public baths in Sampson Square where they would catch up with gossip and get clean at the same time!

SPOT THIS!

Roman feet touched this mosaic 2,000 years ago. You can walk across it too, at Yorkshire Museum.

In the 1980s the remains of the ancient Roman bathhouse were discovered beneath a pub.

We named this great city 'Eboracum', which means 'place of yew trees'.

As a treat, Romans would tuck into a plate of pickled parsnips. Delicious!

Bathtime

It took hours to have a bath in Roman times. First, you would go into a hot room called a caldarium to work up a sweat. Then a slave would scrape off the dirt with a strigil. Next came a hot sauna and finally a dip in an ice-cold pool. The slaves worked very hard and didn't get a chance to relax. One of their jobs was to crawl along the sewers clearing out all the waste.

CELT
500 BC

ROMAN
AD 43-410

ANGLO-
SAXON
AD 450-
1066

VIKING
AD 865-
1066

MEDIEV
TIMES
1066
1485

The Emperor's palace was a busy place. Here, an imaginary slave tells us about a typical day.

Erm, are you sure these snails have been stewed?

Ssshh! My master is sleeping! Before he wakes up, let me tell you a little bit about me...

My name is Marcus and I'm a slave boy. I work in the palace of the emperor Constantine the Great and I'll be honest with you – I was very nervous when I was told I would be working here. The emperor is a powerful soldier and likes things done properly. Luckily for me, he treats his slaves well. I know other slaves who get whipped for making even the smallest mistake.

There's a feast today and everyone is very excited. There are people coming from countries I've never even heard of. You can tell they're important by the expensive coloured robes and the jewellery they wear. Whenever there is a big feast, and that's quite often, I help serve the food. Do you fancy boiled pig stuffed with sausage and black pudding or a plate of stewed snails? No, me neither!

After the feast, the Emperor is going to watch the gladiators fight, but we'll have to stay to clear up. I wish I wasn't a slave – I hear great stories about the gladiators but have never been allowed to go and see them.

This skeleton was 1 of 80 found at The Mount in York. Archaeologists think it belonged to a Roman gladiator!

Eboracum was a large and important city in Roman times.

TUDOR
1485-1603

STUART
1603-1714

GEORGIAN
1714-1837

VICTORIAN
1837-1901

MODERN
TIMES
1902-NOW

How do we know?

When wealthy Romans died, some of their favourite things were buried with them. Over 100 years ago, the skeleton of a woman from Roman times was found in Bootham. Inside her tomb there were two bracelets, a mirror, earrings, beads and a glass jug. That woman has since become known as the 'Ivory Bangle Lady'.

Tests on the lady's skeleton show that she was born in Africa. People used to think that anyone from Africa who lived in Britain during the Roman times was a slave, but the Ivory Bangle Lady has shown that is not true. People came from all over the world to live in the Roman city of York.

Between 2005 and 2006, archaeologists also discovered 80 skeletons in The Mount. They were young, male and many of their heads had been chopped off. At first it was thought they were Roman soldiers who had been executed. Then archaeologists found a bite mark on one of the skeletons, believed to be from a lion, tiger or bear. They now think those men were gladiators!

These objects were found in the Ivory Bangle Lady's grave.

Experts studied the Ivory Bangle Lady's skull to work out what she looked like.

CELT
500 BC

ROMAN
AD 43-410

ANGLO-
SAXON
AD 450-
1066

VIKING
AD 865-
1066

MEDIEV
TIME.
1066
1485

A Viking Raid

1st November, AD 866 begins like most other winter's mornings in York but life in the city is about to change forever. There are huge longships sailing up the River Ouse, like no ships anyone has seen before. No one knows who spotted them first, but word of the invaders soon spreads. Some say they have axes and others say they have swords. The Vikings have arrived.

Seafarers

After the Romans left York, the city came under the rule of the Anglo-Saxons, whose name for York was 'Eoforwic'. The city became important once again. St Peter's School was founded in AD 627 and the very first Minster was built the same year. An archbishop came to live in the city in AD 735 and a monastery with a famous library was built. The Anglo-Saxons weren't strong enough, however, to fight off the next invaders.

The new invaders were the Vikings from Scandinavia. They were a nation of great ship builders and sailors, and every summer another fleet would set off in search of treasures abroad. To find out which way to go, Viking sailors would sometimes release ravens. The birds flew towards land and the longships would follow them. York, which they renamed Jorvik, was one of the many places settled by Vikings throughout the world.

Viking longships had a dragon's head at the front, which Vikings hoped would keep evil spirits away.

Jorvik Takes Shape

The Vikings had a frightening reputation. The sight of them made many people quake in their boots! But the Vikings were also great engineers and businessmen. In York they built a bridge over the River Ouse, repaired the Roman walls and added new streets of houses. York became the second biggest city in the country after London.

SP☉T THIS!

The Jorvik Viking Centre is full of interesting Viking objects. If you go, look out for this carved limestone grave cover.

Many of the Vikings had unusual names. There was Harald Bluetooth, Ivar the Boneless and Sihtric the Squinty!

This comb was used to get rid of Viking headlice! It has its own special case.

Metal helmets like this one made the Vikings look even more ferocious.

They call me Bloodaxe. I fled to England and became King of Jorvik.

A Man Called Bloodaxe

Eric Bloodaxe was a bad-tempered man who lived up to his name. When his older brother was about to be named King of Norway, Eric killed him in the hope of taking his place. Unfortunately for Eric, not everyone liked the idea of having a murderer on the throne and he fled to England. Eric was named King of Jorvik and Northumbria in AD 947 and for the next seven years caused nothing but trouble. However, when Eric died in battle in AD 954, the Viking rule of York ended.

CELT
500 BC

ROMAN
AD 43-410

ANGLO-
SAXON
AD 450-
1066

VIKING
AD 865-
1066

MEDIEV
TIMES
1066-
1485

Viking York was a very smelly place to live in. Rubbish was thrown into backyards where it was left to rot. Imagine the stench of old fish heads, boiled cabbage and mouldy carrots!

Read this imaginary account of Viking York from a young carpenter. Would you have liked living in York during Viking times?

If that's music then my name is Eric Bloodaxe!

The Vikings liked music and carved panpipes from small blocks of wood.

My name is Alvis and I work as a carpenter. It's true what they say: you can smell a Viking from a long way off! But if you don't mind sharing your house with a family of fleas, life's not all bad...

Our homes have walls made of wood and mud, known as wattle and daub. The roofs are thatched and in the centre of the hut there is space for a fire which we use for cooking and heating. We use candles made from animal fat which can make the hut very smoky, but you get used to it.

We spend a lot of time at home and like most of my friends, we have a workshop in the backyard where I work with my dad. I'm learning to be a carpenter but I know some really brilliant craftsmen, who make everything from beautiful glass beads, carefully stitched leather boots to carved wooden bowls.

It's not all work, work, work. We Vikings also know how to party! Some evenings we gather round storytellers and listen to old adventure stories that have been passed down through the generations. There is usually lots of music and singing. I've been practising some new tunes on my panpipes but I'm not very good. I am very skilled at playing boardgames though, especially a game called hnefatafl.

Most Vikings washed in buckets of cold water or took a quick dip in the river. Holes were dug in the ground for toilets.

TUDOR
1485-1603

STUART
1603-1714

GEORGIAN
1714-1837

VICTORIAN
1837-1901

MODERN
TIMES
1902-NOW

We learned lots about Viking York from a huge dig at Coppergate in the 1970s.

Many of the items found at Coppergate are now at the Jorvik Viking Centre, such as this Viking sock.

How do we know?

In Viking times, Coppergate was the street of the cup makers. A thousand years later, developers decided they wanted to build a new shopping centre on the land. Archaeologists knew that it had been an important historical site, but even they couldn't believe what was found.

More than 40,000 separate items were uncovered at Coppergate which helped experts build up a detailed picture of life in Viking York. The moisture in the earth had prevented many of these items from decaying. They found combs made from antlers, and glass beads and leather boots that had been worn more than a thousand years before. They dug up a helmet decorated with animals, discovered in a wood-lined pit. They also found tiny fruit pips and the bones of small animals – evidence of what the Vikings ate. They even found bits of wool that had been used as toilet paper!

The Vikings captured the city and made Jorvik their capital of northern England.

11

CELT
500 BC

ROMAN
AD 43-410

ANGLO-
SAXON
AD 450-
1066

VIKING
AD 865-
1066

MEDIE
TIME
1066-1

Norman Conquest

York is ringing to the sound of hammers and chisels. Workmen are unloading stone for the new Minster and architects are huddled over their carefully drawn plans. The city is determined to show off its wealth and the skill of its craft workers to become the envy of the world. It's a busy time for York.

William the Conqueror

During medieval times, York became very wealthy. However, along the way there were lots of gruesome battles. One particularly famous battle was started by William the Conqueror.

William was a duke from Normandy in France. In 1066, he came to England to fight King Harold. After defeating Harold at the Battle of Hastings, William was crowned king. He turned his attention to the north and arrived in York with hundreds of soldiers. The city tried to put up a fight, but William's forces were too strong.

Two Castles

To show just how important he was, William ordered two castles to be built in York. The first was where Clifford's Tower stands now and the second was just the other side of the river. A seventh of all the land in the city was cleared to build William's giant palace, surrounded by a huge moat known as the King's Pool.

The king's palace might have been impressive but William's plans caused a lot of anger in the city. By the time it was finished, many ordinary homes had been destroyed and several important buildings had been flattened to the ground. This wasn't a happy time for people in York.

William the Conqueror had two castles built in York. Baile Hill is all that is now left of the second castle.

...1066 WILLIAM CONQUERS ENGLAND...1068 WORK BEGINS ON CASTLE IN YORK

TUDOR
1485-1603

STUART
1603-1714

GEORGIAN
1714-1837

VICTORIAN
1837-1901

MODERN
TIMES
1902-
NOW

The Minster

William the Conqueror had destroyed so much of York that the city had to be rebuilt. A man called Thomas of Bayeux, who became the city's archbishop in 1070, led the way. He ordered the building of a new minster and, over the next 400 years, York was transformed. Everyone wanted to create buildings more impressive than those that had gone before. In 1220, work began on the Minster as we know it today.

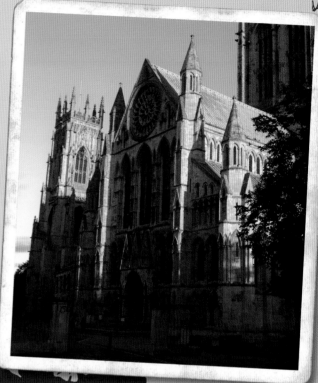

Thousands of men worked on York Minster. It took 250 years to build!

SPOT THIS!

Soldiers stood guard on the city walls. Can you see the murder holes in Monk Bar, where boiling water could be poured down on attackers?

The east window of York Minster is the largest surviving medieval stained glass window in the world!

The Golden Age of York

York wasn't just an important centre for religion. It was also a very wealthy trading city. When King John came to the throne in 1199, he spent a lot of money fighting wars. Desperate for funds, in 1212, King John told the people of York that they could govern themselves in return for a small fee. It meant the merchants became the most important people in the city. They collected the taxes and made all the major decisions.

Much of York's wealth came from the wool trade, but there were lots of other crafts and manufacturing businesses. Each one was controlled by a special group called a guild, and many built their own impressive headquarters, such as Merchant Taylors Hall, to do their business.

A tax collector called Snarrus worked in medieval York. His expensive ivory seal suggests he was a very wealthy man.

CELT
500 BC

ROMAN
AD 43-410

ANGLO-SAXON
AD 450-1066

VIKING
AD 865-1066

MEDIE
TIME
1066-1

Medieval York is famous for the Mystery Plays. Each play was put on by a different guild of workers. The shipwrights performed the building of Noah's Ark, the goldsmiths became the three kings and the bakers performed the Last Supper. This imaginary account from an actor explains more about the plays.

The Mystery Plays are the oldest dramas in the English language and were performed for around 150 years.

It's the day of the Mystery Plays and I've been so excited I haven't slept a wink. Medieval life is hard, but the one thing everyone looks forward to is the Mystery Plays. They are performed each year on the religious feast of Corpus Christi and it's a great celebration. There are 48 plays in total and they tell the stories from the Bible.

All the plays are performed on wagons, called pageants, and each one is pulled through the city's streets. The first pageant sets off from Holy Trinity Priory in Micklegate at 4.30 in the morning! They stop off at 12 different places along the route and there's always a big crowd waiting to see the performance. The actors playing the lead roles do get a bit nervous but with good reason. People who don't know their lines or who look bored on stage are fined!

By the time the sun sets everyone is exhausted and the pageants are packed away for another year.

We must follow the star of Bethlehem!

The Middleham Jewel is a pendant held at Yorkshire Museum. It is engraved with religious figures and its original owner probably believed it had magical powers.

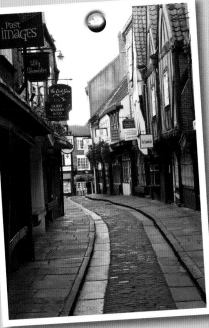

The Shambles was home to 26 butchers in the 15th century.

Bad Times

> Medieval times were a mixture of good and bad for York.

It wasn't all splendour in medieval York and most of the ordinary people didn't live like kings. The city's narrow streets had open drains running through them. Animals were allowed to wander freely. Some said the smell and filth in York was the worst in the whole of England!

The city was also full of rats, which was bad news for York. Rats carried bubonic plague, known as the Black Death. It was a terrible disease and killed almost everyone who got it. The first epidemic hit York in 1349, and before the end of the century it had returned five times, killing thousands of people.

How do we know?

Many of York's medieval buildings are still standing today for us to see and touch. Next time you walk along the pretty Shambles, notice how the pavements are raised above the cobbles so medieval butchers could wash away blood and animal remains in the street!

Many cities had their own version of the Mystery Plays, but the ones in York are thought to be the best preserved. The scripts were forgotten for hundreds of years until the 19th century, when they were republished. The scripts were so good that in 1951, the Mystery Plays were brought back as part of the Festival of Britain. The festival aimed to help boost British morale after World War Two. An original copy of the York Mystery Plays is looked after by the British Library in London. Experts believe it was written in the 15th century.

CELT
500 BC

ROMAN
AD 43-410

ANGLO-
SAXON
AD 450-
1066

VIKING
AD 865-
1066

MEDIE
TIME
1066-1

Horrible Henry

Trouble is brewing. Henry VIII has ordered his soldiers to take control of England's monasteries. St Mary's Abbey is one of the first on their list. Rumours are spreading that the king's troops are getting nearer. Nuns and monks are living in fear and their quiet peaceful lives are about to be destroyed forever.

York versus Lancaster

In the late 1400s, England was at war as two noble families, the House of York and the House of Lancaster, battled for power. The war came to an end in 1485 at the Battle of Bosworth when Henry of Lancaster won and became King Henry VII. This was bad news for York as it meant the city was seen as less important.

York's businesses struggled and there was more trouble ahead. In 1509, Henry VII died and his son, also called Henry, became king. At first Henry VIII was popular but, like many kings, he liked his own way.

No More Monasteries

England had been a Catholic country for hundreds of years and everyone, including kings and queens, had to obey the Pope. Henry was married to Catherine of Aragon but he wanted a new wife – one he hoped would give him a son. When the Pope said Henry VIII couldn't get divorced, Henry announced he was going to start his own church. This was known as the Reformation. Life became very dangerous for people who did not worship in the new Protestant way.

With other Catholic countries threatening to invade England, Henry VIII needed money to build a large army. The Catholic church had been very wealthy, so he decided to take the riches from the monasteries. In York, St Mary's Abbey was the first to be raided. The monks were made homeless and, as Henry's troops went on the rampage, many of the city's religious buildings were destroyed.

↰ Henry VIII ordered St Mary's Abbey to be destroyed.

...1485 LANCASTER WINS BATTLE WITH YORK...1539 ST MARY'S IS DESTROYED.

 TUDOR 1485-1603

 STUART 1603-1714

 GEORGIAN 1714-1837

 VICTORIAN 1837-1901

 MODERN TIMES 1902-NOW

Margaret Clitherow

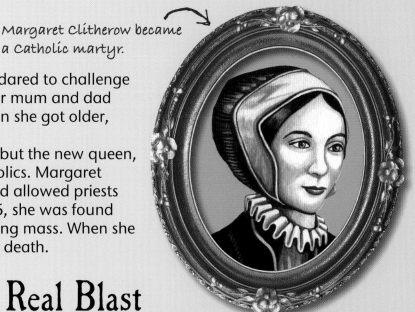

Margaret Clitherow became a Catholic martyr.

A young woman called Margaret Clitherow dared to challenge the new Protestant religion. Born in 1556, her mum and dad belonged to the Church of England but, when she got older, Margaret decided to become a Catholic.

Henry VIII had been dead for some years, but the new queen, Elizabeth I, also punished troublesome Catholics. Margaret secretly taught children the Catholic faith and allowed priests to hide in her house in the Shambles. In 1586, she was found guilty of helping Catholic priests and attending mass. When she refused to reject her faith she was crushed to death.

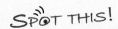 SPOT THIS!

Can you spot this plaque on Ouse Bridge? It marks the place where Margaret Clitherow was put to death.

A Real Blast

Guy Fawkes also died because of his beliefs. He went to St Peter's School in York and as he grew up he became very angry about how Catholics were being treated. In 1605, Fawkes and a group of friends plotted to blow up the Houses of Parliament. They hoped the current king, James I, would be killed in the blast. Fawkes wanted to light the fuse, but on 5th November he was caught and sentenced to death.

Remember, remember, the fifth of November...

The cellars of the Houses of Parliament are checked every year to make sure no plotters are hiding there!

Bonfire Night is also called Guy Fawkes Night, after this Yorkshire schoolboy.

Rich people took pride in being fashionable in Tudor times. During the reign of Elizabeth I, the men dressed even more elaborately than the women!

This imaginary account is from a Tudor girl called Anne, whose father is a wigmaker. Anne is talking about what life is like for poor people in York.

I want to own over 80 wigs, like Queen Elizabeth!

York is very rich these days. The city's royal links attract many wealthy visitors who love to spend money. The streets are filled with shops selling gold and silver jewellery and fine embroidered dresses. My dad makes wigs and he has so many orders he doesn't know what to do. All the noblemen and their wives wear wigs and they are desperate to keep up with the latest fashions.

My dad says sometimes he doesn't recognize the city any more and he's not too keen on all the inns that have opened. He says ale rots the brain!

We are lucky because we're quite well off, but not everyone is rich. Some people can't even afford to eat so they walk around the street in rags, begging for money and food. The men in charge of the city don't like beggars and have passed a new law to keep the numbers down. Some have been allowed to stay but they have to wear tokens around their necks so everyone knows who they are. Anyone spotted begging is sent out of the city or given jobs no one else wants to do.

There's so much more I could tell you but I've got to go. A cock-fighting competition is about to start and I want to get a seat right at the front!

Tudor men's clothes gave them a square shape, to make them look big and powerful. Women wore clothes to make them look triangular and feminine.

TUDOR
1485-1603

STUART
1603-1714

GEORGIAN
1714-1837

VICTORIAN
1837-1901

MODERN
TIMES
1902-NOW

Royal Visitors

Charles I came to York to escape trouble in London!

While many lived in fear when the Tudor and Stuart monarchs were on the throne, life wasn't all bad for the people of York. England had 12 different kings and queens in almost 220 years and many of them visited York and saw the city as an important base for keeping the north of the country under control. In 1642, Charles I, who wasn't very popular, even moved the royal court from London to York to escape the mobs who were threatening to overthrow him.

How do we know?

Coats of arms were only given to the most important places and, in 1587, Queen Elizabeth I gave York one of its very own. The arms can be seen all over the city. They are usually made up of the red cross of St George, which symbolized the city's religious importance, and five gold lions, which represented York's support of the royal family.

At King's Manor, the coat of arms of Charles I can also be seen. The inscription, Dieu et Mon Droit, is written in French and means, 'God and my Right'. Henry VIII, Charles I and James I all stayed here.

The Tudors and Stuarts loved visiting York!

King's Manor is now part of the University of York.

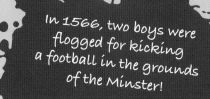

In 1566, two boys were flogged for kicking a football in the grounds of the Minster!

19

CELT   500 BC

ROMAN AD 43-410

ANGLO-SAXON AD 450-1066

VIKING AD 865-1066

MEDIEVAL TIME
1066-1485

Highways to Railways

It's pitch black when the carriage of a wealthy nobleman suddenly jolts and stops. Everyone knows what it means. Dick Turpin is about to strike again. Waving his pistol, the famous highwayman orders everyone to hand over their jewels and money. The robbery is over in minutes and then, as he's done so many times before, Turpin disappears on his black horse, galloping off into the night.

Money, Please!

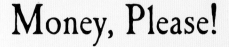

During the 18th century York continued to be a popular place with the rich and wealthy. They went dancing at the Assembly Rooms, attended feasts at the Mansion House and always looked their best for race days at Knavesmire. It was a prosperous time for the city, but money brought its own problems and those riding in and out of the city became a target for highwaymen.

The highwaymen weren't dashing outlaws, but violent criminals. The most infamous of them all was Dick Turpin. After shooting and killing a man, Turpin fled to Yorkshire, where he was arrested for stealing horses. He gave a false name, but his true identity was eventually discovered and, in 1739, crowds gathered on the Knavesmire to watch Turpin being hanged on the gallows. He was buried at St George's Church in Walmgate.

Step inside Dick Turpin's cold and creepy cell at York Castle Prison, now a museum.

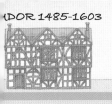

Railway Revolution

Aside from the occasional highway robbery, Georgian York was fairly quiet. But in Victorian times the pace of life quickened and even the highwaymen could not keep up. Everyone knew the arrival of the railways would mean a big change for the city and finally, in 1839, the wait was over.

The excitement had been building for months. Hundreds of people gathered to watch the large locomotive crank into life. The noise was incredible and, in a cloud of steam, the very first train pulled out of York.

Fairfax House is a fine Georgian house in York. Go inside to discover how wealthy Georgians lived.

Famous authors such as Charles Dickens visited York to read extracts from their latest books.

Another George

George Stephenson built the first railway line from Newcastle to London. A man called George Hudson persuaded him to run the track through York, making York the centre of the new rail network. This made Hudson very popular and he became known as the 'Railway King'. But, in 1849, Hudson was accused of bribing MPs to increase his empire and he soon lost his millions. The York solicitor who exposed Hudson was George Leeman. He became very important and made sure York stayed at the centre of the railway network.

Champions of Chocolate

The railways brought industry to York. Raw ingredients such as cocoa beans and sugar could now be transported from the other side of the world, and two large factories, employing thousands of people, began churning out chocolate bars. One factory was owned by Joseph Rowntree and the other by Joseph Terry.

Joseph Rowntree wasn't interested in just making himself wealthy. He gave half of his money away to charity and at New Earswick he built an entire village for his workers where they had access to a library, doctor, dentist and free education.

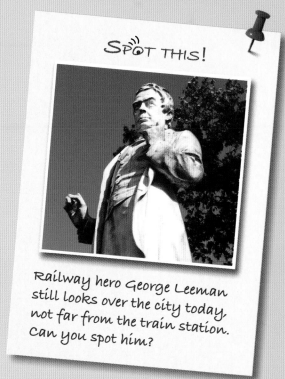

SPOT THIS!

Railway hero George Leeman still looks over the city today, not far from the train station. Can you spot him?

Thousands of people were employed at the chocolate factories to come up with new ideas for sweets, work the giant machinery and, best of all, taste the final product. The imaginary account on the right is from a worker at the Rowntree's factory in the late 19th century.

This photo of Joseph Rowntree was taken in 1925.

Once a Rowntree's warehouse, this building is now a block of luxury apartments.

When I was little I dreamed of working in a chocolate factory. Then it happened. I was 14 years old, left school on the Friday and started at Joseph Rowntree's factory on the Monday. My mum, dad and older brother were already working there. In fact most of the people I know work there!

It's a big place and takes at least 10 minutes to walk from one end of the site to the other. I work in the 'chocolate beans' section, putting the packets into boxes so they can be sent away to sweet shops.

As my mum always tells me, I'm lucky to have a job. Back when she was little, there wasn't much work around for women. Besides, Mr Rowntree is a kind man and Mum says there aren't many of those around either.

I must not eat the chocolate. I must not eat the chocolate.

You have probably heard of the Chocolate Orange but did you know that the first chocolate fruit to be made by Terry's was a chocolate apple?

Dirty Slums

While those who worked in the chocolate factories had quite a good standard of living, for many people in Victorian York life didn't smell so sweet. Home for many families was just one room in a slum and the tiny amount of food they could afford was washed down with dirty water from the nearby well. The very worst off were sent to the workhouse where they were given a bed but little else. Diseases were common and many children died from pneumonia, typhoid or measles.

Kirkgate Street is a life-sized model of a Victorian street inside York Castle Museum.

This Victorian cab was invented by a local man called Joseph Hansom.

Not much happened in Georgian York but in Victorian times the city grew really fast.

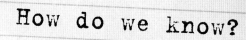

How do we know?

Born in 1869, Dr John Kirk was a Yorkshire doctor and a keen historian. He wanted to let future generations know how people had lived in the past and so, in the 1930s, he started the York Castle Museum. In it, he built a typical Victorian street, complete with a chemist, sweet shop and pawnbroker, where people would swap their goods for money. He also built a small courtyard with a second-hand clothes shop and cheap grocer's to show where the poorest people would have shopped.

York at War

York is fast asleep when the sirens begin to sound. German planes are heading towards the city. Children are carried from their beds into air-raid shelters, and for the next few hours families huddle together listening to the explosions as their homes and workplaces burn.

New Arrivals

In World War One, many men would have left York to join the armed forces. But during World War Two, lots of people arrived in the the city. Many children were evacuated to York and nearby villages as the government thought they would be safer here. Lots of foreign airmen also came to the city and often spent their time off in Betty's café.

A bombed street in York in 1942

A Perfect Target

For the first few years of the war, York escaped the bombings which had destroyed many parts of England. In April 1942, its luck ran out. English airmen had bombed two ancient cities in Germany, destroying many of their medieval buildings and half-timbered houses. The German forces wanted revenge. Flicking through a guidebook known as Baedeker they decided York, with its historic streets and impressive old architecture, was the perfect target for their bombs.

Many men left York to fight in the world wars.

...1939 WORLD WAR TWO BREAKS OUT...1942 YORK IS BOMBED IN BLITZ...

TUDOR
1485-1603

STUART
1603-1714

GEORGIAN
1714-1837

VICTORIAN
1837-1901

MODERN
TIMES
1902-NOW

April, 1942

People had grown used to the noise of the air-raid sirens. For two and a half years they had been practising evacuation drills, but this night, they soon realized it was the real thing. Seventy German planes swooped across the city, dropping their bombs on Coney Street and the Bar Convent School. The attack, which began at 2.30am, lasted 90 minutes. By the end, 74 people were dead, 92 seriously injured and 113 slightly wounded. Out of 28,000 homes in the city, 9,500 were destroyed.

When the all-clear was sounded, people came out of their air-raid shelters and went to see just how much damage had been done. The pavements were covered with a carpet of glass and rubble, entire buildings had disappeared but, amazingly, the Minster was untouched.

People carried maps showing the location of 23 shelters in York, just in case the city was attacked while they were out shopping.

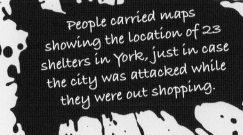

SPOT THIS!

4TH PARA BATT
REG COULTAS
5TH PARA BRIGADE
KEN. RUDDY
6 OCT 1943

Many of the foreign airmen who came to York during the war etched their names on a mirror in one of their favourite places. Try looking downstairs in Betty's café.

Betty's bar and café were very popular with airmen in York during the war.

I recall visiting York Minster when I was a princess, followed by a lovely lunch with the Lord Mayor.

Pulling Together

The whole of York was helping with the war effort. Rationing meant there was no point making sweets, so instead Rowntree's chocolate factory began making munitions and dried egg for ration packs. Their chewing gum department was turned into a secret fuse factory. The Germans had hoped the attack would crush people's spirits. But it didn't work. Many people whose homes were destroyed went to work as usual the next morning and one woman, whose home had been badly damaged, refused to leave until she had found a duster to clean up with!

CELT
500 BC

ROMAN
AD 43–410

ANGLO-
SAXON
AD 450–
1066

VIKING
AD 865–
1066

MEDIEV
TIME
1066
1485

Foods that were hard to get hold of were rationed during the war. Rationing made sure food was shared out fairly. In the imaginary account below, Elsie talks about how rationing affected her brother's birthday party. Elsie is eight years old and lives in York.

Each week, every person was given about 110 g lard or butter, 340 g sugar, 110 g bacon or ham and two eggs.

Mum, do I have to wear this? It smells worse than Edward's feet!

My name is Elsie and yesterday it was my brother Edward's 10th birthday. We had a small party but there was no chocolate or fancy sandwiches. They've just brought in rationing and that means we can't eat what we want any more. Everyone has a book with tokens in it, which we swap for things like butter, ham and eggs.

Sometimes my dad tells me and Edward about the great big party we're going to have when the war is over. He's promised us that as soon as rationing is lifted he'll buy us a big bunch of grapes and a bag of oranges, washed down with a big cup of tea. I don't like tea but the grapes and oranges sound good.

Since the Germans bombed York I've been scared to go to bed in case they attack again. We've got an Anderson shelter in our back garden, but I don't like it much in there. It's cold and the gas masks we have to wear smell funny.

Mum says I should remember how lucky I am. Some children in big cities have been separated from their parents and evacuated to the countryside to live with other families. I don't think I'd like that.

York Castle Museum has all kinds of wartime objects, including gas masks and ration books.

Betty's was nearly closed down in 1943. This letter helped to save the café.

12th August, 1943

Dear Sir,

We acknowledge receipt of your letter dated 11th August with very great concern. We must point out that we serve an average of 20,000 (twenty thousand) Main meals, Subsidiary meals, Teas and Hot beverages, per week. In addition we are retailers of bread and flour confectionery. The Bars are also popular and are largely patronised by the forces.

We maintain that we perform an essential public service in York and we sincerely hope that you will not find it necessary to commandeer the establishment.

We trust to be favoured with an interview at your convenience.

Yours faithfully,
BETTY'S (HARROGATE) LTD.,

Lieut. Colonel,   Chairman and Managing Director.
Quartering Command No. 5 Area,
1, Queen's Road,
Harrogate.

It's 1945 and these workers from Betty's are all smiling because the war is over.

How do we know?

There are lots of photographs and newspaper reports about the bombings. "Bootham was a sight to make the historian weep," wrote one reporter. "Glass, glass everywhere crunching under our feet. Every house had empty windows, tiles off the roof and the walls were all pitted with machine gun bullets."

Many of the American airmen also left their mark on Betty's café, writing their names on a mirror, which still hangs on the wall today.

When World War Two was over in 1945, a lot of people wanted to forget about what happened. The British soldiers who came home found it difficult to talk about the things they had seen when they were fighting. However, over the years people have been encouraged to write down their own stories of the war. Some have written entire books about what happened and others have had their memories recorded on websites.

After World War Two, a lot of York had to be rebuilt.

York Today and Tomorrow...

Evidence of York's past is everywhere to see, from the towering Minster to the narrow street of the Shambles and its ancient city walls. Archaeologists are carrying out new digs all the time, to help piece together an even clearer picture of what life was like in the city hundreds and even thousands of years ago. But what will experts of the future think about the way we live today?

The medieval Mystery Plays are still performed around York today. Have you seen them?

The Jorvik Viking Centre is built on exactly the same spot where the Coppergate digs took place.

There are over 1,000,000 historical objects to see at the National Railway Museum in York!

Each year, hundreds of Vikings descend on York for a re-enactment of the battles and to show people the kind of food that Vikings ate. Do you think there will ever be a festival celebrating how we live today?

Each year, thousands of students come to York's universities. Science City York has been set up to create new jobs in 21st century businesses. What jobs do you think people will have in the 22nd century?

York's city walls are the most complete medieval walls in England. Do you think they should always be there?

The Shambles was recently voted the most picturesque street in the whole of Britain!

SPOT THIS!

Look out for five lions around the city. York's coat of arms is still used today by the council. Can you remember which queen gave York this coat of arms?

How will they know?

As well as digging below ground and looking through dusty paper records, archaeologists and historians of the future will be able to look through online records. In 100 years' time, will an expert be looking at something you posted on the Internet?

Just like the Romans and the Vikings, we might not realize it, but we are already leaving our mark on history. From the clothes we wear to the games we play and the food we eat, someone, some day, could well be reading about how we live now.

You should feel proud to be a part of York's future.

Today, Terry's and Rowntree's chocolates are popular around the world.

Glossary

Abbey – a building where monks or nuns live and work.

AD – a short way of writing the Latin words anno Domini, which mean 'in the year of our Lord', i.e. after the birth of Christ.

Air raid – a type of attack using planes to drop bombs. Air raids occurred during World War Two when German planes bombed Britain. Air-raid sirens warned people that planes were coming.

All-clear – when an air raid was over and it was safe to leave your shelter, another siren sounded. This was called the all-clear.

Anderson shelter – a covered shelter, often in gardens, where people went for protection when bombs fell during World War Two.

Archaeologist – a person who studies the past by examining buildings and objects left behind by previous people and cultures.

Blitz – the attack by German planes on British towns during World War Two.

Catholic (or Roman Catholic) – a member of a Christian religion headed by the Pope.

Christianity – a religion whose followers believe Christ is the son of God.

Church of England – a Christian religion headed by the king or queen.

Evacuate – to leave home and move to a safer place to live.

Fort or fortress – a large, strong building offering military support and protection.

Georgian era – the time from 1714 to 1830 when any of the four kings called George reigned in England.

Gladiator – a man in Roman times who was trained to fight in the arena for entertainment. Gladiators often fought to the death.

Guild – an organization of craft workers and traders. A Guild protects the rights of its members and the prices of their goods.

Highwayman – a masked robber who waited on roads for travellers to come along, then stole their money and jewellery.

Hnefatafl – a Viking boardgame similar to chess.

Monastery – a place where monks live and worship.

Monk – a male member of a religious community that has rules of poverty, chastity and obedience.

Plague – a disease that spreads easily and can kill. In medieval times, a plague could wipe out thousands of people. It was also called the Black Death.

Protestant – a member of the Christian religion that considers the king or queen to be the head of its church.

Ration book – a book recording how much food you were allowed every week. Ration books were used during World War Two when certain foods were scarce and had to be shared fairly among everyone.

Slum – a very poor part of a city that is run-down, dirty and often overcrowded with people.

Stonemason – a person who works with stone and makes things from it.

Victorian – a person or thing from the period of time when Queen Victoria ruled.

Workhouse – a place where poor people lived and worked when they had nowhere else to go.

Index

Acknowledgements

The author and publishers would like to thank the following people for their generous help:
A huge thank you to Jackie Logan and the Yorkshire Museum for kindly allowing photography, and to Ben Young for providing images from the Jorvik Viking Centre. We are also very grateful to Betty's & Taylors of Harrogate and everyone at Betty's bar and café tea rooms in York.

The publishers would like to thank the following people and organizations
for their permission to reproduce material on the following pages:
p5: York Museum Trust (Yorkshire Museum); p6: York Archaeological Trust; p7: copyright Aaron Watson, University of Reading; p9: York Archaeological Trust, www.jorvik-viking-centre.co.uk; p10: York Archaeological Trust, www.jorvik-viking-centre.co.uk; p11: York Archaeological Trust, www.jorvik-viking-centre.co.uk; p13: York Museums Trust (Yorkshire Museum); p14: York Museums Trust (Yorkshire Museum); p18: Mary Evans Picture Library, Alamy; p20: York Museums Trust (Castle Museum); p22: Getty Images; p23: York Museums Trust (Castle Museum); p24: Trinity Mirror/Mirrorpix/Alamy; p25: Betty's & Taylors of Harrogate; p26: York Museums Trust (Castle Museum); p27: Betty's & Taylors of Harrogate; p28: Imagestate Media Partners Limited, Impact Photos/Alamy, Richard Peel/Alamy.

All other images copyright of Hometown World

Written by Sarah Freeman
Educational consultant: Neil Thompson
Local history consultant: Allison Freeman
Designed by Stephen Prosser

Illustrated by Kate Davies, Dynamo Limited, Mike Hall, Tim Hutchinson,
John MacGregor, Leighton Noyes, Nick Shewring and Tim Sutcliffe
Additional photographs by Alex Long

First published by HOMETOWN WORLD in 2011
Hometown World Ltd
7 Northumberland Buildings
Bath BA1 2JB

www.hometownworld.co.uk

Copyright © Hometown World Ltd 2011

pb ISBN 978-1-84993-147-2
hb ISBN 978-1-84993-124-3

Your past
Your now
Your future

Your history4ever

Mmm... Still love chocolate pudding!

My next one's going to have 2 wheels!

Trophy for the trendiest glasses?

I love you too!